READING KEYBOARD MUSIC

The Work of C. W. Reid (revised)

Volume Two

edited by

Martha Miner

Lulu Cheney

Julianne Dent

Kathleen Bauer

Copyright 1988, 1991, 1994 Demibach Editions
7883 North Pershing Avenue, Stockton, CA 95207

ISBN 1-881986-14-4
ISBN 1-881986-16-0

C.W. Reid was the originator and composer of this unique course of beginning keyboard study. Born December 1, 1872 in Manti, Utah, he taught piano from the age of eleven years until his death in 1959.

C.W. Reid was the chairman of the Music Department at Brigham Young University, Provo, Utah, and later professor of music at the McCune School of Music in Salt Lake City.

He retired in 1931 to teach privately. He gave the remaining years of his life to developing and perfecting his inspired system of sight reading and technic. These ideas had come to him after much searching and experimentation to find a more effective way to approach beginning keyboard study.

RKM

Instructions for Volume Two

Learning to read music quickly is an enormous encouragement to the beginning keyboard student. READING KEYBOARD MUSIC is unique in that it teaches note reading by using *Place Specific Names* which relate visual and tactile patterns on the keyboard to the patterns on the music staff.

The emphasis of this method is on learning to read music quickly. Consequently, the method does not contain familiar tunes as these encourage playing by ear and guessing as to note placement. This method also uses the minimum of finger numbers in the pieces. Finger numbers are given only for hand placement. Students must then rely on reading notes, not finger numbers, to play a piece.

READING KEYBOARD MUSIC, **Volume Two**, introduces treble clef ledger notes. It is divided into five *Units*. Each *Unit* contains:

- **New Information:**
  The information on the *Rhythmic Definitions* page and enclosed in boxes at the top of the page is critical to the students' understanding of music. Take time to teach this information carefully.

- **New Pieces:**
  Discovering repetitive or similar patterns within a piece enhances the speed with which a piece can be learned. Take time to discover any obvious patterns with the student prior to playing a new piece.

  Beginning pieces in **Volume Two** are written on a single treble clef staff to facilitate note reading. *Stems up* indicate right hand and *stems down* indicate left hand. Music written on a double treble clef staff is introduced in *Unit 2*. Bass clef is introduced in **Volume Three**.

- **Written Exercises:**
  The *Written Exercises* drill note placement on both the staff and keyboard thus further reinforcing note reading. These exercises are to be completed before progressing to the next unit. If more written exercises are required, **Written Work Papers** are available from the publisher.

  Letter names on the keyboard are introduced in Unit 3. When introducing letter names on the key board, have the student become familiar with the visual pattern CDE-FGAB.

- **Technical Exercises:**
  Mastery of the *Technical Exercises* at the end of each unit is critical to the ability to play music well. Note reading progresses so rapidly that without consistent practice of these exercises, the fingers will not be able to execute what the mind can read and comprehend.
  Review all *Technical Exercises* weekly.

- **Rhythmic Drills:**
  Careful consideration needs to be given to the rhythm of each piece before beginning to play it. *Rhythm Drills* in the back of this volume correspond specifically to the pieces in **Volume Two**. These *Rhythm Drills* highlight the concept of the underlying beat while drilling the rhythmic pattern of the piece. If more rhythm drill is required, **Rhythm Flash Cards** are available from the publisher.

- **One Minute Test:**
  The *Note and Pattern Review* on page 44 is to be used as a test to determine the students readiness to begin study in the next volume. Once the student can play this page in approximately one minute, proceed to **Volume Three**. At this point, **Volume Two** and **Volume Three** may be taught at the same time. For younger students, 6-8 years old, preparatory work in the **Young Beginner Workbook, Volume Three**, is recommended.

TABLE OF CONTENTS

Reading Step 1

> ***Ledger notes*** are notes written above or below the staff.

The *three space notes below the staff* and the *three space notes above the staff* form the same keyboard pattern.
The *three space notes below the staff* are located adjacent to *bottom line* and *bottom space*.
The *three space notes above the staff* are located adjacent to *top space* and *top line*.

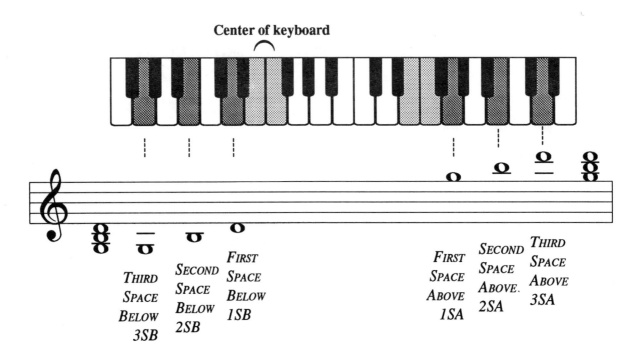

Play and name the following notes:

The *two line notes below the staff* and the *two line notes above the staff* form the same keyboard pattern.

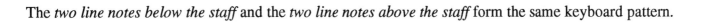

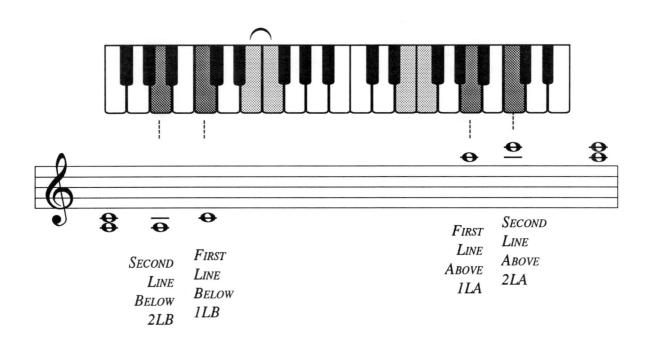

SECOND
LINE
BELOW
2LB

FIRST
LINE
BELOW
1LB

FIRST
LINE
ABOVE
1LA

SECOND
LINE
ABOVE
2LA

Play and name the following notes:

Study 1

Preparatory Exercise:

New Neighbors

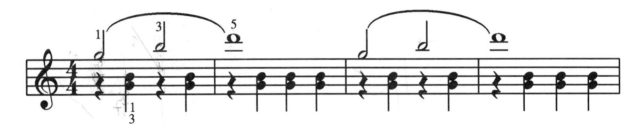

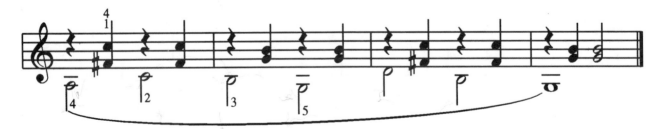

Study 2

Swing High, Swing Low

Andante (a slow walking tempo)

Written Exercise 1

Write the note number on the keyboard as indicated.
Next, play and names these keys.

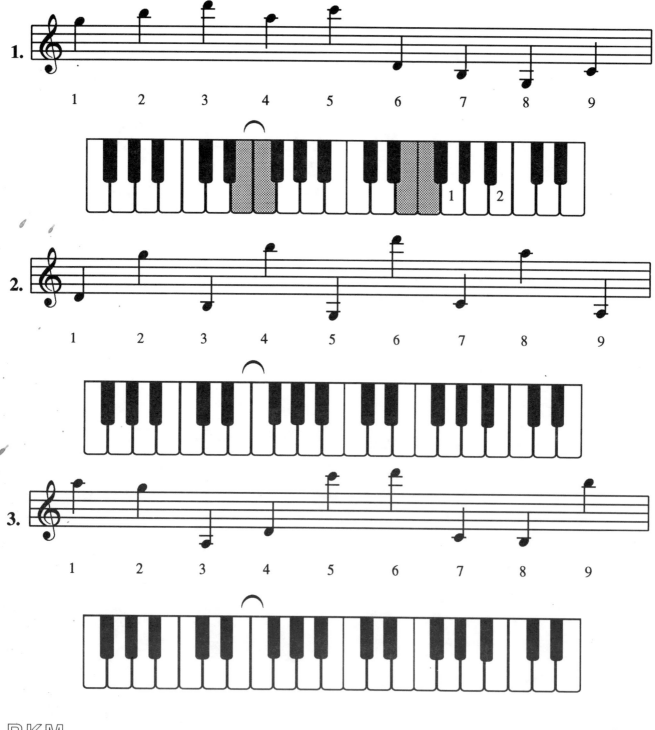

Technical Exercise 1

This exercise is to be learned by rote.
Use the keyboard and graphic below as a reminder of hand placement.
The notes above the finger numbers on the keyboard show the starting place for this exercise.

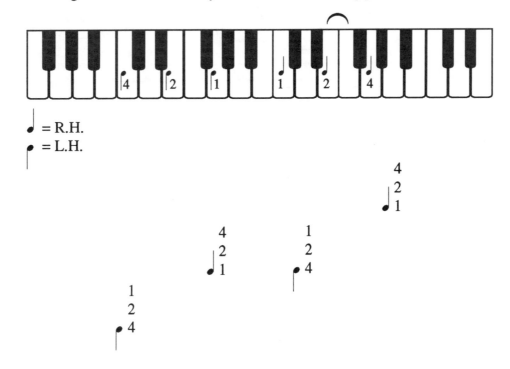

Play this exercise on eight consecutive keys.

Alternate fingering, $\begin{smallmatrix}5\\3\\1\end{smallmatrix}$ may be used throughout these chords.

For teacher only: This exercise is to be taught by rote.

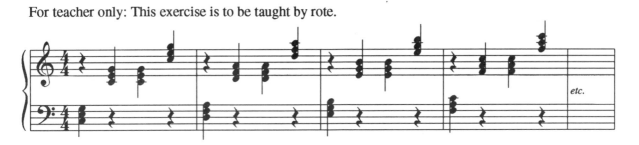

Study 3

Piano II

Moderato (medium tempo)

Note to teacher: This piece may be played as a duet on one piano by playing the student part one octave higher than written.

Study 3

April

Moderato (medium tempo)

Study 4

A *staccato* dot above or below a note means to release the key quickly.

Legato means to play in a smoothly connected manner.

Holiday

Allegretto (moderately fast)

Study 5

Calliope

Allegretto (moderately fast)

Written Exercise 2

Study the abbreviations on the following keys.
Next, play and names these keys.

Write the appropriate abbreviations on the following keys.
Next, play and names these keys.

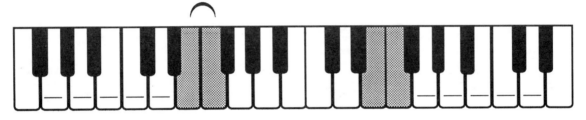

Write the notes above the abbreviation as indicated.

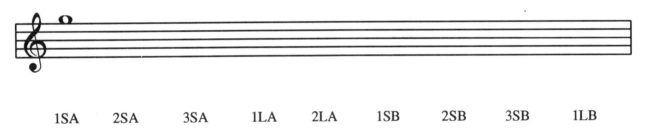

Write the abbreviations below the notes as indicated.

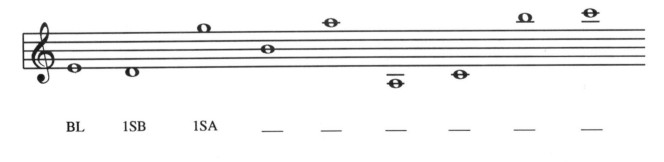

Technical Exercise 2

This exercise is to be learned by rote.
Use the keyboard and graphic below as a reminder of hand placement.
The notes above the finger numbers on the keyboard show the starting place for this exercise.

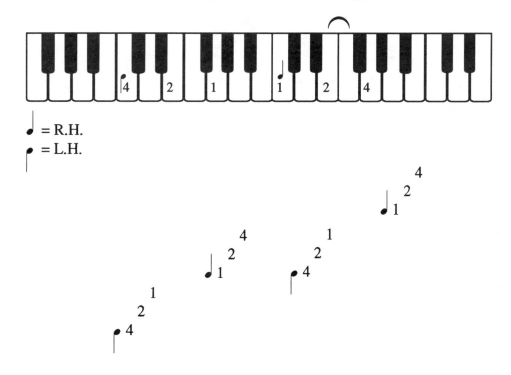

♩ = R.H.

♩ = L.H.

Play this exercise on eight consecutive keys.

Alternate fingering, $\begin{matrix} 5 \\ 3 \\ 1 \end{matrix}$ may be used throughout these chords.

For teacher only: This exercise is to be taught by rote.

Study 6

Two *eighth notes* last as long as 1 quarter note. (♩)

Carousel

Allegretto

Study 7

A *half rest* is a sign for silence lasting as long as a half note (𝅗𝅥) or two quarter notes. (♩ ♩) Notice that it sits on top of middle line.

Snappy Fingers

Animato (lively)

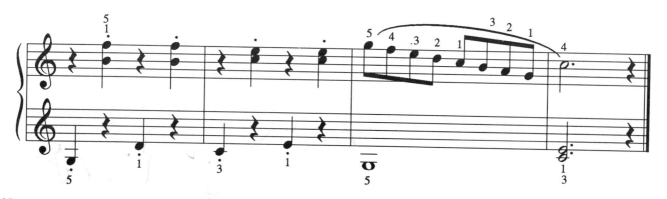

Note to teacher: At this point, have students begin playing the **One Minute Test** on page 44.

RKM

Study 8

Secondo

Study 8

Ping Pong

Animato

mf

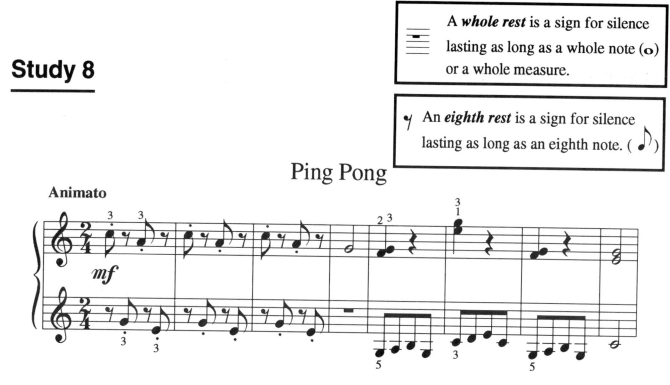

Written Exercise 3a

To help in communicating about music, *keys* are given letter names: A-B-C-D-E-F-G

Write all the CDE's by the two black key groups on the keyboard below.

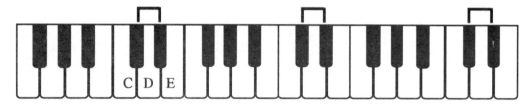

Write all the FGAB's by the three black key groups on the keyboard below.

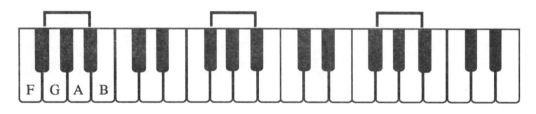

Write all the CDE's on the keyboard below.

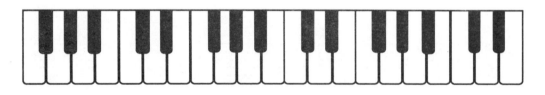

Write all the FGAB's on the keyboard below.

Written Exercise 3b

Write all the D's in the two black key groups on the keyboard below.
Play all the D's on your keyboard.

Write all the C's and E's by the two black key groups on the keyboard below.
Play all the C's and E's on your keyboard.

Write all the G's and A's on the keyboard below.
Play all the G's and A's on your keyboard.

Write all the F's and B's on the keyboard below.
Play all the F's and B's on your keyboard.

Written Exercise 3c

Write all the letter names on the following keyboards.

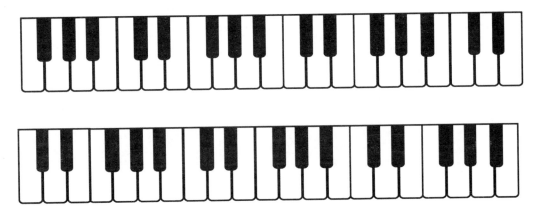

Write the note number on the keyboard as indicated.

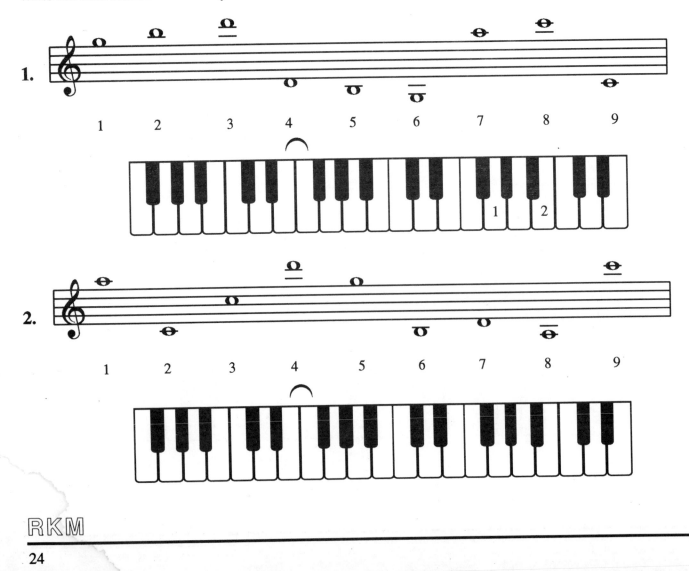

Technical Exercise 3

This exercise is to be learned by rote.
Use the keyboard and graphic below as a reminder of hand placement.
The notes above the finger numbers on the keyboard show the starting place for this exercise.

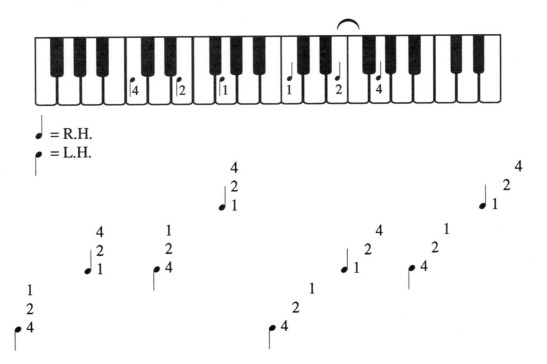

♩ = R.H.
♩ = L.H.

Play this exercise on eight consecutive keys.

Alternate fingering, $\begin{matrix} 5 \\ 3 \\ 1 \end{matrix}$ may be used throughout these chords.

For teacher only: This exercise is to be taught by rote.

etc.

Study 9

Scamper

Secondo

Allegretto

Study 9

Scamper

Study 10

Folk Dance
Secondo

Study 10

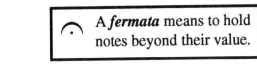

Folk Dance

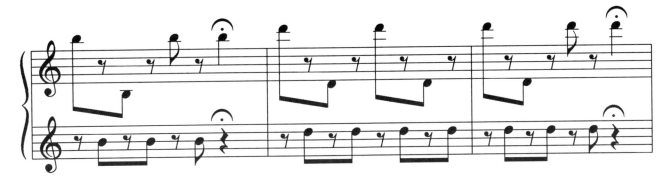

Written Exercise 4

Notes written **above** the middle line have stems down on the left.

Notes written **below** the middle line have stems up on the right.

Notes written **on** the middle line can have stems either direction.

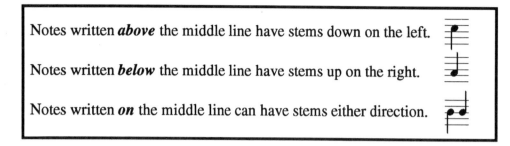

Write the notes on the staff as indicated.
Use the following abbreviations to indicate
the rhythm value of the note:

1 = quarter note (♩) 1 beat

2 = half note (♪) 2 beats

3 = dotted half note (♩·) 3 beats

4 = whole note (o) 4 beats

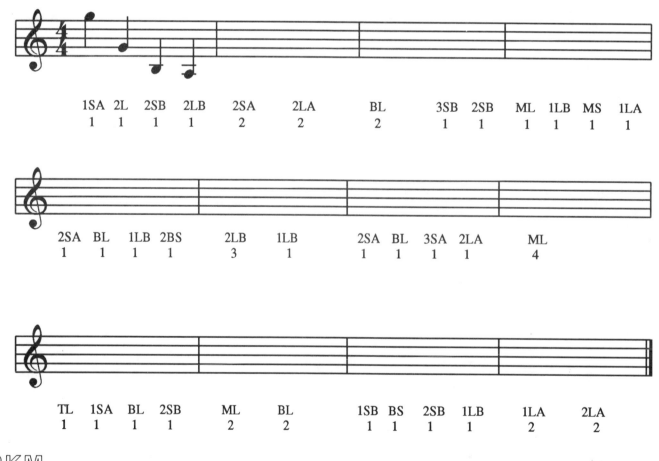

| 1SA | 2L | 2SB | 2LB | 2SA | 2LA | BL | 3SB | 2SB | ML | 1LB | MS | 1LA |
| 1 | 1 | 1 | 1 | 2 | 2 | 2 | 1 | 1 | 1 | 1 | 1 | 1 |

| 2SA | BL | 1LB | 2BS | 2LB | 1LB | 2SA | BL | 3SA | 2LA | ML |
| 1 | 1 | 1 | 1 | 3 | 1 | 1 | 1 | 1 | 1 | 4 |

| TL | 1SA | BL | 2SB | ML | BL | 1SB | BS | 2SB | 1LB | 1LA | 2LA |
| 1 | 1 | 1 | 1 | 2 | 2 | 1 | 1 | 1 | 1 | 2 | 2 |

Technical Exercise 4

This exercise is to be learned by rote.
Use the keyboard and graphic below as a reminder of hand placement.
The notes above the finger numbers on the keyboard show the starting place for this exercise.

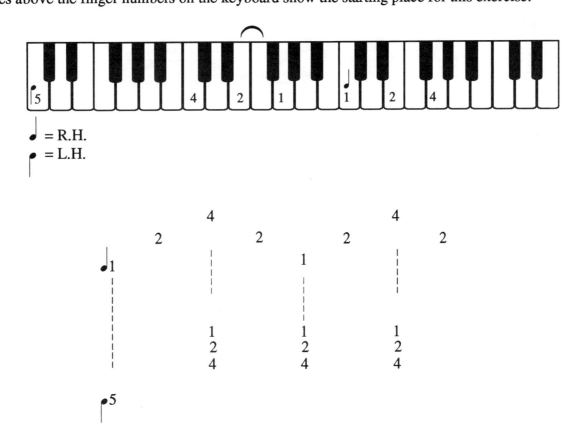

Play this exercise on eight consecutive keys.

Alternate fingering, $\begin{array}{c} 5 \\ 3 \\ 1 \end{array}$ may be used throughout these chords.

For teacher only: This exercise is to be taught by rote.

Study 11

Ghosts and Goblins
Secondo

Study 11

Ghosts and Goblins

Misterioso

Study 12

Cloudy Weather
Secondo

Moderato

Fine

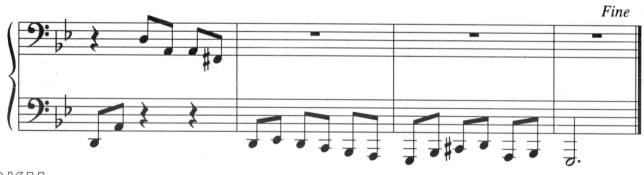

Study 12

Cloudy Weather

Fine

Study 12

Cloudy Weather
Secondo continued

D. C. al Fine

Study 12

Cloudy Weather
continued

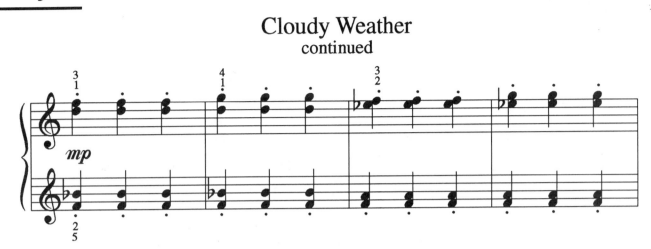

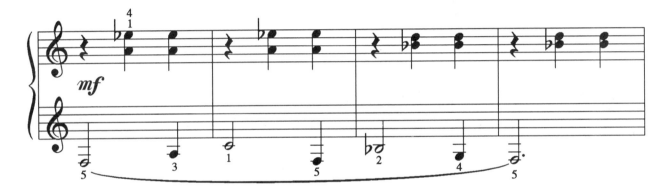

D. C. al Fine

Written Exercise 5

Write the note number on the keyboard as indicated.

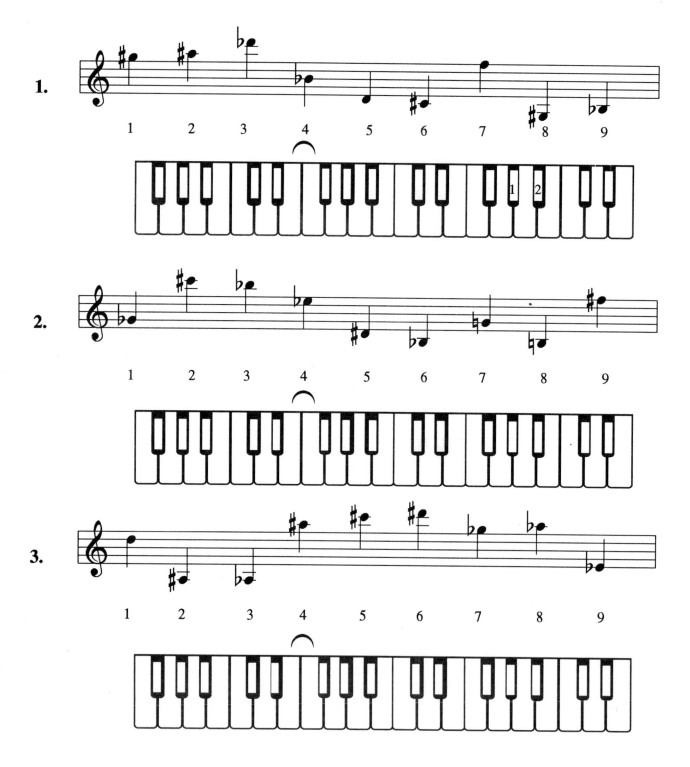

Technical Exercise 5

This exercise is to be learned by rote.
Use the keyboard and graphic below as a reminder of hand placement.
The notes above the finger numbers on the keyboard show the starting place for this exercise.

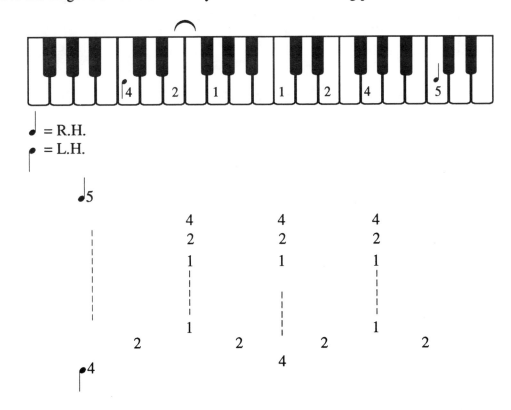

Play this exercise on eight consecutive keys.

Alternate fingering, $\begin{smallmatrix}5\\3\\1\end{smallmatrix}$ may be used throughout these chords.

For teacher only: This exercise is to be taught by rote.

RKM

Rhythm Drills

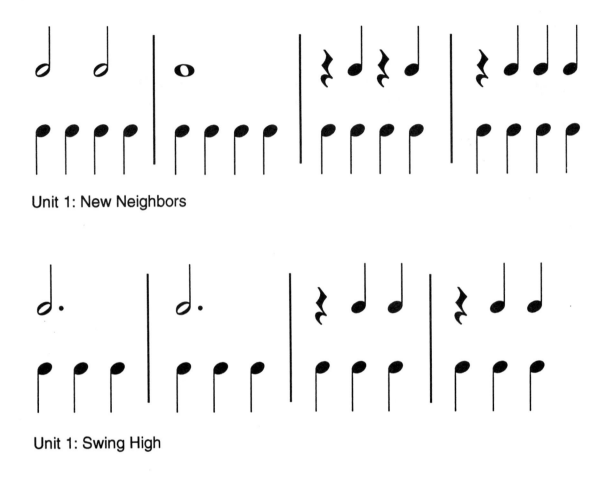

Unit 1: New Neighbors

Unit 1: Swing High

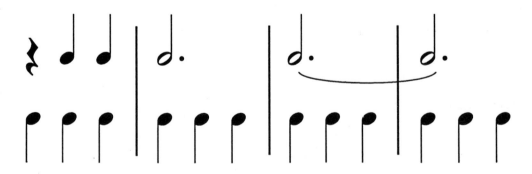

Unit 2: April, Holiday, Calliope

Note to teacher: Before beginning to play a new piece, drill the above patterns. The student claps the pattern (top), while the teacher claps the beat (bottom).

RKM

Rhythm Drills

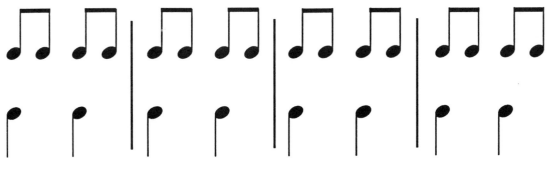

Unit 3: Carousel

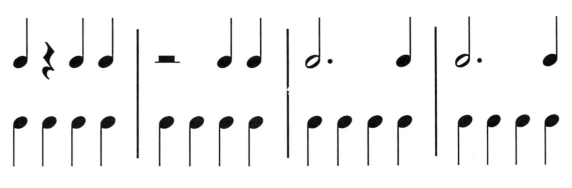

Unit 3: Snappy Fingers

Unit 3: Snappy Fingers

Rhythm Drills

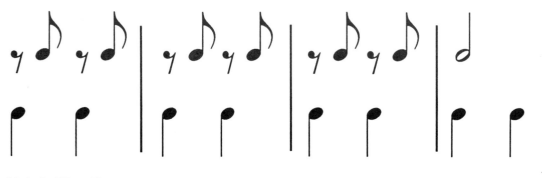

Unit 3: Snappy Fingers

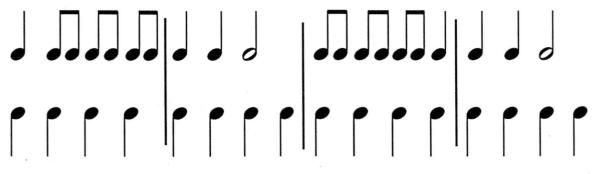

Unit 3: Ping Pong

Unit 4: Scamper

Rhythm Drills

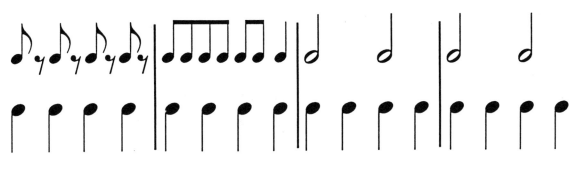

Unit 4: Folk Dance

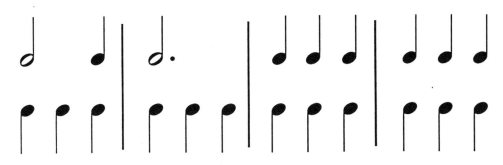

Unit 5: Ghosts and Goblins

Unit 5: Cloudy Weather

One Minute Test

Practice these note and pattern reviews until they can be performed in one minute or less.

Note to teacher: This note and pattern review is to be used as a timed test beginning with Unit 3. When the student can play this page in approximately one minute, proceed to **Volume Three**. At this point, **Volumes Two** and **Three** may be taught at the same time.

Note Review:

Pattern Review: